Peter Podmore

Cold Breeze, Dark Fire

Bizzle Arts

ISBN 978-0-9557055-0-2

Published by Bizzle Arts
5 Westnewton
Wooler
Northumberland
NE71 6XJ
www.peterpodmore.co.uk

Printed and bound by
Martins The Printers Limited
Berwick-upon-Tweed

Design by www.simprimstudio.com

Acknowledgements

To the Northumberland National Park Authority for their generous assistance in the production of this book.

To Jenny and Simon Court for all their help and support, and to John and Kate Hersey at Unison Colour.

Tors in Winter

Frost from Heaven
The devil's fingers
Numb on moaning strings

Old Nick's trill
Whistled by angels
Who crack the ice
Under their stamping feet.

A bleating trumpet
Nips his wind-pecked ear,

Stiff, fallen wings dismiss
In suffering gusts
Lucifer's wheezing, ectoplasmic breath

And fan
To white, bright frozen heat
The starched and golden fire.

Peter Podmore

Introduction

The North of Northumberland is an outstandingly beautiful area of England relatively undiscovered, where traffic moves freely, and where one can walk for hours without meeting a soul. Neolithic hill top forts are still grazed by wild goats, standing stones and circles sit untroubled in farmers' fields and ancient stones abound etched with strange, uncomprehended cup and ring marks – Roughting Linn, Old Bewick, Lordenshaws and Doddington and many more, burial places – possibly – of an ancient world. The fields and hills are scarred with the agricultural workings and terracing of more than two thousand years ago. The air, apparently, is the least polluted in England and at night the bright canopy of stars closes down on the dark looming shapes of the hills from the blackest of brilliant black skies. The night air is shot through with the sound of tawny owls and oystercatchers. The land teems with roe deer, pheasant, grouse, partridge and hares and, at dusk, badgers and barn owls emerge into the darkening landscape with the foxes and otters. I live dangerously. Bulls use my easel as a scratching post. I have been savagely and repeatedly attacked by a pheasant, mounting my painting table and trying to seize the brush from my hand. And I was nearly run over by a short sighted roe deer. Stoats kill rabbits before my very eyes, sparrow hawks hurtle past in pursuit of prey and buzzards wheel expectantly overhead mewling like cats.

Simonside Moors 2005 Pastel 36x50cm
Private Collection

But, as a painter, the real joy of this landscape is its great variety, from the purple moors and the orange brackened hills to the lush lowland greens, the rivers, lakes and huge sandy shores. There are castles and priories and old stone farm buildings. The light is clear, cold and bright, quite different from the soft, damper and warmer light of the West and Cumbria.

There is the sense of isolation, of being in a relative wilderness where one can be completely alone and undisturbed., the fantasy of a city-locked population driving the streets in their spotless 4x4's, imagining – only imagining. In an age which, like the Industrial Revolution, is increasingly urban centred, affinity in the towns with the wild and the cultivated outdoors tends to be circumscribed by romantic preconception and sentimentality. This incomprehension is reinforced by the more escapist and idealised 'postcard' landscape images perpetuated by marketing and the media. I try to communicate a landscape of mud and wind and cold and sun, the landscape I live in that I see changing with every day, a landscape far more beautiful than any Photoshopped photograph could ever idealise.

This natural space that I inhabit is a crucial part of the psyche of a population that I am sure is trying to reconcile the artificial, virtual reality of a constructed environment with the increasingly strident political buzzword of the moment –'green'. The value of the open spaces of North Northumberland is incalculable - even if it only exists in peoples' imagination. Knowing it is there…

This is not a topographical guide to the well-known parts of North Northumberland It is the measure of my pleasure in being part of this extraordinary panorama of ever changing light and atmosphere and my interest in recording my thoughts and feelings in the passing of the days and merging of the seasons. I continually hope that my own observations will bring others to new ways of looking at the landscape, its light, its space, its colour.

How I work

The problems of working outside have been catalogued by artists down the centuries – bright sunlight reflecting on the page, working in one's own shadow, maintaining stability in a wind and, in winter, generally keeping warm enough to think clearly. Battling with the elements , while not always comfortable, can bring the most exciting painting rewards.. Pastels have great advantages in that they do not reflect light in the way that oils do, they do not have the drying problems of watercolour and, once good operating colours have been identified, they can be worked very quickly and transported easily. Turner, who rarely painted out of doors, did pencil sketches, complaining to someone who wanted him to work in colour that he could do 15 or 16 pencil sketches in the time it took him to do one oil sketch. However he also used to say that his best outdoor paintings were done in under half an hour. For me, as for Constable and Turner, speed also is of the essence in order to capture a particular moment of passing light and hold it in the mind's eye. Cézanne, who worked outside in the south of France on paintings for two months at a time, gave himself other problems to deal with. In Northumberland in that time the whole character of the landscape would have changed unrecognisably to a searching eye. Thank goodness Cézanne does not appear to have had to deal with suddenly blossoming fields of bright yellow rape.

As far as possible I prefer to do most of my work in the open air. I stand always at an easel with a board and paper, sometimes a canvas, and I work quickly in pastel, using chunky thumb-sized pastels made in Northumberland by Unison Colour, which withstand vigorous application and whose colours are closely related to the landscape. I work on a soft-sized velvet or satin Somerset paper, 250 gsm, on which I can move the pastel around, rub it down with kitchen paper and rework it. I start with a single dark colour that reflects the underlying colour of the subject, and then work freely to provide an energetic ground for the drawing that explores the main structural dynamics, general tonality and proportions of the drawing. I build up the colour using as few pastels as the situation will allow to keep the colour relations strong and the work as simple as possible. Given that the light is changing all the time and with it my subject matter, in the middle of the day when the light is more stable I can work on the drawing for up to an hour and a half, maybe two hours. Later in the day I have to work faster for an hour or less. I can usually reach a point where, although the work is not completely resolved, I can clearly identify with that ineffable quality and point of particular visual interest that I set out to understand in my drawing.

When I bring the drawing into the studio my main concern is to establish the underlying abstract strength of the work and to clarify and harden that special presence and quality that I had identified from the beginning. A good drawing guides the eye through a series of relationships and the way that the relationships connect is entirely dependent on the construction of the image. The eye subconsciously draws imaginary lines between various points – of complimentary tones, colours, shapes and so on – and the structure is built up of verticals, horizontals, diagonals and arcs that control the special reading of the image. Verticals and horizontals relate to the flat surface of the picture bounded by its rectangular frame that we call the picture plane. Diagonals tend to lead the eye through the picture plane, like perspective. In making any adjustments to the work it is these 'lay lines' that have to be cleared and any unnecessary interruption to the flow of perception of the piece removed. The way the drawing operates can be quite complicated and not immediately apparent. It can take a long time to understand and it may be on the wall for weeks before I find a simple resolution to the problem.

Ardnamurchan from Glengorm 1995 Pastel 35x49cm

As a simple illustration, in the pastel drawing of Ardnamurchan, the work consists of four horizontal features – sky, land, sea, land – which take the eye across and relate the drawing the to the picture plane. In other words they make the drawing feel flat. However there is a much more subtle diagonal starting from the bottom right corner and passing through the two highest points in foreground and background and this offers a countervailing sense of depth to the picture in the absence of any clear perspectival features to take the eye into the background.

There are some drawings which present very clear, fairly simple but interesting structural propositions and these I sometimes work into paintings in the studio. I am using the paint to explore other ways of manipulating the imagery through having to work with a fluid material which can be built up into a relatively textural statement. The two different processes ask questions of each other and sometimes I find I am trying to translate a working method in oils, say, into new approaches in the medium of pastel. On the whole oil painting, because it is more studio bound, is much more difficult and takes a lot longer. Many paintings have been worked on for a number of years. They go back into the store when either I can be deluded into thinking they are

Willows, Fence and Stream 2004
Oil on canvas 120x100cm

tremendously successful, or I cannot see a way forward with them. They are then revisited some months later when the scales have fallen from my eyes. And so the process continues.

To make clearer the way the structuring process works, in the painting of Willows and Stream it is fairly clear how the flatness of the picture plane is being attacked by, for example, the line of fence posts which make a secondary illusory plane taking the eye back into the picture. Another plane is created by the posts coming in from the left. Yet another goes from the front post through the second tree to the top point of the stream. So the internal space of the image is carved up by a series of intersecting planes and directional statements. They form a series of irregular rectangles that interlock and contradict each other, each suggesting a perspectival reading very much in the way that the abstract folded paper piece is working. The weight of the tonal statements, the darks and the lights and the shapes of the stream and the trees are controlled within this visually unstable and optically interesting conflict of directional leads.

Titian was the great master of working planes within the picture plane. Degas used the tilting plane of the floor to give his works their dynamic. Manet's paintings are all very carefully constructed so that you could pass a ruler over any one of them and all the most significant highlights of the work join up along verticals, horizontals and diagonals. This is what, in quite an inconspicuous way gives all these painters' works their strength, their dynamic.

Every mark or shape or gesture asks a question which has to find an answer in another part of the work. Like a sudoku puzzle, everything has to fit. The energy, the sense of transience, the overall speed of a painting or drawing is controlled by the structure not by mere gestural handling of the medium. A lot of agitated application of paint does not necessarily make for an active painting.

However I do not believe it is necessary to analyse every painting in this way to have an understanding of it, any more than it is necessary to understand the engine to enjoy a ride in a car. I am simply explaining the principles of the way that I work for the benefit of those who might wish to understand them perhaps for their own artistic purposes.

Drawing and painting is about relationships between colours, tones, images, surfaces and other mechanical instruments of painting, but all these elements are subservient to the understanding of space. The function of any work operates through the realisation and manipulation of relationships in space, the questioning tension between one mark or image and another. I cannot remember who said that 'music is not the notes but the sound between the notes'. It corresponds to the drawing class mantra to 'draw the space between the objects not the objects themselves'. The organisation of space and spatial relationships are the emotional keys to the works expression.

Why I Paint Landscapes

How I look at landscape is central to how I paint it. The central paradox that guides my work is that I am trying to look at nature objectively, a nature that has no visual rules of its own that seems in essence quite anarchic in the way that it presents itself to the human eye, and yet I have to contain that visual experience in an image that relates to a particular way of seeing, conditioned by the rectangle of the picture plane. I can talk about describing the energy of light and wind, of the rambling outlines of hills and the complex twisting and turning of the willow trunks, but I have to explain them through a kind of neo-geometrical structure which, while explaining the force of my experience, may be completely at odds with how they would look to the casual observer. The process appears quite self-contradictory. Yet the extraordinary point is that whenever I am struggling to reconcile structurally different points of the drawing, there is always something I can find in the subject matter that I have overlooked. I can always find an answer to the problem by looking a bit harder at what I am trying to draw. I am never sure whether I am imposing selectively a structure of my own, or whether, as I suspect is more likely, the natural structure is already there. Is the anarchy, the haphazard appearance, simply a front, or, is it, on the other hand, that the reason for my approaching the drawing in the first place was that I had identified a natural incident on which I could impose my own rules of composition?

There's nothing more real than trudging over wet, muddy hills with cold hands and bitter rain driving into one's face. It is a solid, tangible experience. But the act of looking at the natural phenomenon playing so directly on the sensory experience is quite another thing. The hills can loom, darken, come forward, retreat and merge with the sky. Clouds play fast and loose with the scenery, the light never lets it stand still. The landscape appears as an ever changing illusion. And yet somehow the artist has to magically capture his response to this vision that will explain it as an occurrence in a moment of time. I can do no better here than quote Cézanne: '*All that we see dissipates moves on. Nature is always the same, but nothing of her remains, nothing of what appears before us. Our art must provide some fleeting sense of her permanence, with the essence, the appearance of her changeability*'. That contradiction, '*some fleeting sense of permanence*' and simultaneous '*changeability*', is what my pictures are about.

It is also one of my biggest technical problems. How Cézanne managed to express that impermanence, in his long, carefully explained paintings for me is an imponderable. I may take up to an hour in one place to find a subject. I am waiting for the moment when, with a particular shift of the light, perhaps, I am confronted with an unexpected change in the spatial relationship of two or three areas – the space opens up when light falls on the yellow grass behind a tree, darkening the tree and throwing it into sudden relief, or the relative configuration of trunks of willow suddenly become intriguing. The process is not a rational one, it is not always possible to explain what I have seen, but I have to respond intuitively and quickly before the moment passes - in an hour, if I am lucky. I never set out to paint a hill or sea or sky, I paint what is happening to that hill, sea or sky.

For seventeen years after leaving Art College at Farnham in 1976 I worked in an abstract format looking at problems of space and spatial contradictions. I was concerned with the way a simple geometric statement could be looked at in different ways from different angles – the 'Eats Shoots and Leaves' dilemma. In a strange way I had always regarded these pieces as resolved when I felt a presence of landscape creep into the work. One day, on a walk between Langleeford and Goldscleugh under the Cheviot, I looked at a valley bathed in sunlight being suddenly transformed by a passing cloud into a dark, cavernous fold – something I had noticed many times before but it had never made such a strong impression on me. The idea that light can change shape and form and sensation was something that I tried to explore for a time more fully in my abstract work, until I suddenly felt the need to address this problem much more directly by going out into the landscape itself and bearing witness to the phenomenon by drawing in the open air. I also felt I had spent enough time dreaming up and constructing problems out of my head, and that I needed to spend time looking again and digesting external information. My days of landscape painting alternated with life drawing sessions in the studio.

The more landscape painting that I did, the more focused I became, and aware of the inexhaustibility of the subject matter. The land was throwing back to me new colours, new spatial questions, and new structural problems such as I could never have devised sitting in my studio working things out mathematically and in my head. I was becoming involved in the work in a completely different way and a way that I enjoyed. Because everything had to happen so quickly, I was having to respond intuitively yet investigatively at the same time. The seascapes took me back to my minimalist roots, based on simple horizontals and subtle diagonals. The closer work (on the willows, for example), led me into the problem of how to look into a complex space where forms pass in front of one another and have to be looked through. A camera focuses on one level to separate object from background or, it may, using depth of field, present an undifferentiated record which provides no distinction between individual parts of the image. But it works with a mechanical eye and in my experience offers very little insight or explanation. It may tell a good story but the process of drawing provides the opportunity of a much higher degree of selection, analysis. and thoughtful exposition.

In drawing I can think in almost musical terms where lines of music and layers of sound are organised over each other – like a Bach three part invention. There is a continuous interweaving in music between the parts that takes place in a linear sequence of events in time.. Painting, however, takes place in a moment of time. The trick is to lead the eye such a merry dance through and around the space created that the work can express something of its place in time, a sense of imminence and its role in the continuity of existence. I want the energy of the work, standing outside with the wind blowing and the sun dancing, to reflect the feeling that something else is about to happen, the world is in the process of change.

Folded Paper 1992 Pastel and charcoal 43x38cm

Willows and Steading 2003 Oil on canvas 100x120cm

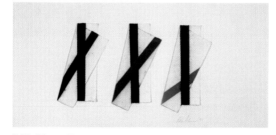

Folded Paper Triptych 1992 Pastel and charcoal 27x58cm

The Valleys

The Coast

Westnewton

43

Introduction

The Valleys

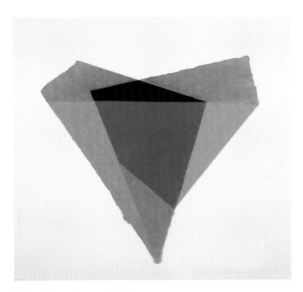

Folded Linen Paper   1992
Pastel and charcoal on linen paper   50x50cm

The Coast

Westnewton

Snow at Westnewton 2007 Pastel 51x70cm

Biography

Having studied literature, history and philosophy in Londonderry and at Trinity College, Dublin in the sixties, Peter Podmore spent some years teaching before taking a Fine Art degree at West Surrey College of Art in Farnham from 1972 to 1976. He emerged from Farnham with an interest in minimal and constructivist principles in painting and showed in Holland and Poland and widely throughout the British Isles. His work was acquired by the Gemeentemuseum in The Hague and the Pushkin Museum, Moscow. He moved to Newcastle upon Tyne in 1979 and in 1991 completed an MA in Fine Art at the University of Northumbria.

In 1993 he began painting landscapes and moved up to Westnewton on the Scottish Border in 1995. His landscapes are shown regularly in the Newcastle area and across Northumberland, and from London to Cumbria, Scotland and the Isle of Mull. They are in many private collections and in the House of Lords.